Heathen Massive Blue Line

Quite a Journey for Hell to Hear

Just for Today with Erotomania Love Addiction

Yvonne Patricia Stewart-Williams

chipmunkapublishing
the mental health publisher

All rights reserved, no part of this publication may be reproduced by any means, electronic, mechanical photocopying, documentary, film or in any other format without prior written permission of the publisher.

> Published by
> Chipmunkapublishing
> United Kingdom

http://www.chipmunkapublishing.com

Copyright © Yvonne Patricia Stewart-Williams

Saturday 23rd February 2013

Dear Yvonne,

Whilst at work this evening at my Thames Reach - Waterloo Project SE1 full time PAYE – pay-as-you-earn Complex Needs and Mental Health Homelessness Charity work, where my specialism is Mental Health and Wellbeing, I received a phone call on my personal mobile phone. At the time, I was busy so I didn't answer it. Later when I noticed that it was from a 'Caller Unknown'. I panicked. The last time this happened r e g a r d i n g C , i n 2 0 11 , i n s i m i l a r circumstances, it was the police. It ended with my being fined, given an indefinite restraining order, a two year conditional discharge with a promise from the judge that I face five years of imprisonment if I re-appeared. In addition, I was given a one year official written warning, following a disciplinary hearing at work, which was held on my file and was only spent in December 2012.

Tuesday 26th February 2013

Dear Yvonne,

I am grateful. I have had no mystery phone calls in the last few days and Grace, my Care Co-ordinator Mental Health Social Worker has not yet called to say the police have contacted her. Thank you, Jesus. So far I have been saved from having another round of unrequited love same sex discussion with my traditional Black Nigerian Mental Health Care Co-ordinator. The fact is I love C. She is a White Sikh, London United Kingdom born European heritage woman. I have adored C exclusively and have remained celibate for almost nine years.

Since my almost two months imprisonment in 2009 for her non-violent harassment, followed by almost three months of locked ward psychiatric hospital impatient stay, nine months on leave from my full- t ime employment, which led to my being redeployed to another post, in Waterloo, Lambeth with a new Specialism of 'Digital Inclusion' for our hostel of all ages adult Criminal Justice System entrenched, parents and none - engaged in multiple varying faiths and none, mixed gender, races, disabilities, education, nationalities and sexuality clients, with multiple poly addictions and alcohol usage, mental health, HIV/AIDS, Hepatitis C and male, female and transgender sex industry and begging employment; with non gender specific sex addiction, and histories of domestic violence and rape. In addition, I experienced a nine month estrangement from my nine year old biological only child; my only contact with C these days is to be frequently perusing her online activities FaceBook; Vimeo; YouTube; Soundcloud; Twitter; plus her Websites and blogs.

Saturday 2nd March 2013

Dear Yvonne,

Today I went to watch the Opera CARMEN at the Royal Albert Hall. I left feeling that was Love Addiction madness to the extreme. I pray, I don't experience it first- hand!

Wednesday 20th March 2013

Dear Yvonne,

It is 13:00hrs. Today is my annual leave off from work and while waiting to attend my 'ACT for Recovery' severe mental illness therapy, I am seated in the Ritzy cafe, Brixton SW2, thinking about my delight with my: True Names King James Version Bible and my Complete King James Bible audiobook.

As two nights ago, this Monday, whilst listening to my favourite online sanctified gospel music by Andy G aka Andrew Grizzle on Radio Plus 101.5 Coventry http:radioplus.org.uk on TuneIn, I was moved. Through music, I felt a deep seated sense of faith. I was close to tears with a true connection with the God of my understanding. I adore my Higher Power and I witness He, She or Its love of me, in so many ways each and every day, one day at a time. My most profound sense of my Spiritual Being's love for me was in 2009, when I was a prisoner in HMP Holloway Women's Prison.

I was seated in the Chapel during prayers and communion with other prisoners, prison guards and chaplain, witnessing prisoners being blessed and holy water applied to their foreheads while prison guards with bunches of keys attached to large chains watched. I was hardened and couldn't allow myself to be blessed and prayed for likewise but felt overcome with an 'Amazing Grace' and the words of the hymn 'saved a wretch like me' came to my heart and mind. I just love the William Wilberforce film 'Amazing Grace' and his eBooks including 'Real Christianity'. William Wilberforce is my all-time favourite countryman.

My all-time favourite American President is Abraham Lincoln. I just love his eBooks of his writings and speeches and the film of him 'Lincoln'. My all time favourite historical American Quaker is John Woolman. I just love his eBook Journal.

Saturday 18th March 2017

Dear. Yvonne,

Yesterday I visited Brixton Cycles with my Brompton Bicycle and sat in the Brixton Cycle cafe sipping a hot beverage, reading a iBook; while my Brompton bicycle was being checked. In the evening I attended a OWF - Order of Women Freemason, Lodge Adelaide Litten No.23 Installation meeting with my Mother Lodge and dined during the Festive Board. Thursday 16th March 2017, after a day at my paid full time work, with my Thames Reach employer, which I have been in full-time paid employment for just about ten years. I started on the 10th April 2007; I attended a CWO - Conservatives

Women's Organisation workshop at CCHQ - Conservative Central Headquarters. I have started taking courses with CWO since taking my Conservative PAB - Parliamentary Assessment Board test in October 2016 and it also being suggested to my during drinks with the LGBT+ Conservatives [Lesbian, G a y , B i s e x u a l , T r a n s g e n d e r + Conservatives].

Wednesday 15th March 2017, Mr Jeremy Swain, my Thames Reach, CEO/Chief Executive - who I follow on 'Twitter' - was in a meeting at my Waterloo Project department. The last time that I saw Jeremy face to face was when we were at

The House Of Lords, where he was speaking on Homelessness and Mental Illness, alongside 'Big Issue Founder Lord

John Bird and Paul Farmer - The CEO/Chief Executive of MIND Mental Health Charity/ Time To Change.

Who I informed and chatted with about my intentions to be the first Openly Lesbian Black Conservative Lesbian Member of Parliament for the United Kingdom, as I am Happy and my long-term monogamous committed sexual same-sex loving relationship with Julian Martin-Findley - [Findlay], who I have known for fifteen years and our love just grew deeper and deeper. Julian and I are Spiritual sisters and we are also best friends. Julian is a Black, Land Owner, Jamaican born

Christian. She is a regular church attender and Sunday school Teacher; in addition to being a very busy Woman Police Detective and trained individual, who is frequently on murder scenes, dealing with rapes and robbery; in addition to also being responsible for driving the police force transport and being present for matters in Courts including Gun Court work… ; Julian is also an extremely active hands on biological birth mother of two sons, conceived during her marriage to a policeman. Julian and me are totally opposite. In November 2016, I took annual leave from work and went on holiday to the Barbados Caribbean Honeymoon 'Sugar Bay' Resort with Julian and my beloved biological teenage son James. On my return, I performed a Stonewall School Role Model presentation talk, about my lesbian sexuality normality to a all girls school in Slough. Mentioning that we now have our second woman Prime Minister; both women have been Conservative party Members, just like me. I believe that as a British Quaker Overseer, responsible for pastoral care - Religious Society of Friends Member at Brixton. I am especially privileged and humbled to have been the Chief Witness of the first ever legal same-sex male wedding to take place during the Westminster Meeting House Meeting for Worship between Roy and Carlos; Sunday 12th March 2017.

I am a OU - Open University student who loves all Apple Products; I am a 'Guy's Hill, Jamaica Land Owner. I am London United Kingdom born and have lived in my Social Housing rented home in Brixton, London United Kingdom, Coldharbour Ward for over ten years.; I stood at the 2010 and the 2014 Local Elections and took part in Hustings at the Karibu Centre opposite Brixton Police Station on Gresham Road, in which I was seated next to the UKIP Candidate, who asked me to vote for him.

I aim to stand at the 2 0 1 8 L o c a l E l e c t i o n f o r m y neighbourhood Brixton Coldharbour Ward and I aim to apply to become a Magistrate at my local Camberwell Green Magistrates Court. I am a published author, my previous eBooks are 'Altered Perceptions' and 'Still On The Cusp of Madness' available on 'Chipmunkapublishing' and 'Amazon'. I regularly food shop in M&S - Marks and

Spencer's; especially in my Brixton neighbourhood and Waterloo, where I work. Prior to riding my Brompton bicycle to work and sometimes after work, I visit my local neighbourhood Ritzy Bar, wearing my Stonewall Rainbow Laces, where I may also watch a film. Work life Balance. I support the 'Brixton Pound' which can be secured in Morley's in Brixton. In addition to my Effra Hall Pub and Library.

Wednesday 26th April 2017
Dear Yvonne,

Today is 'Lesbian Visibility Day' and I am in a Stonewall video film has been launched online by DIVA and Stonewall
https://youtu.be/3lJul3qOWi8

Yvonne Patricia Stewart-Williams

Heathen Massive Blue Line

Saturday 29th April 2017
Dear Yvonne,

Today I completed my online application to try to become a magistrate at my local Camberwell Green Magistrates Court. I have recently booked places for me and my same sex partner Julian to sleep rough for one night at KIA, Surrey County Cricket Club at the Oval on 17th November 2017 for the Big Issue.

I am getting ready for the July 2017 Pride Lesbian, Gay, Bisexual, Transgender and Queer walk with my Thames Reach

Heathen Massive Blue Line

Employers and clients. This will be the first time my Thames Reach Homelessness Charity has taken part in pride and I am one of two staff members who is responsible to feed back to the Thames Reach Diversity and Equality meeting after I attend a Pride Briefing on June 2017; including helping my organisation to organising for the event. I aim to look out for Stonewall on the day.

Naturally I am filled with the June 8th 2017 General Election fever. Call me a bias 'Tory' but I am hoping that Prime Minister Theresa May MP, our country's second Women Prime Minister is given an overwhelming mandate for her negotiation for Brexit…
My twitter is: Yvonne_S_W

Yvonne Patricia Stewart-Williams

Heathen Massive Blue Line

Just for today, one day at a time, I'll end on this: There are a few images which I am not in. One is a photograph which I took of my biological son James with my birth mother Lilian, while out food shopping. The another is taken by me of my beloved son James with my long term lover Julian, on holiday at the 'Sugar Bay Resort' in Barbados. There are also a few others.

Yvonne Patricia Stewart-Williams

Heathen Massive Blue Line

Yvonne Patricia Stewart-Williams

Heathen Massive Blue Line

Heathen Massive Blue Line

Yvonne Patricia Stewart-Williams

Heathen Massive Blue Line

Yvonne Patricia Stewart-Williams

Before I retired from Thames Reach homelessness Charity I wrote and published the Apple book 'My Granny is a drone pilot'. It is a short Childrens book which adults can read which I have dedicated to my grandchildren. I have one grandchild. A granddaughter. She is the bloodline birth granddaughter of my much loved black Jamaican woman Jamaica constabulary Force Police Officer and there is NO woman alive I love more than her. I am a stocks and shares holder and own a few shares in Apple, BP and Marks and Spencer's... to name a few. I was a named director of a few Companies House limited businesses and once held a formal mortgage for a three bedroom London house at 95 Highclere Street, Sydenham. I remain a London born Londoner and usually resident in a housing cooperative rented maisonette in Brixton, Windrush Ward Lambeth; where I resided whilst conducting my lived experience Rethink Mental Illness 'Schizophrenia Commission' commissioner role and Stonewall UK 'Schools Role model' voluntary work. It has also been the address on the ballot paper for all of the elections I stood for within the 'Coldharbour Ward' including my last 2018 By Election. All for The Tory Conservatives.

As of Sunday 3rd July 2022; during a time when we yesterday celebrated the 50th London Pride Anniversary and I have been formally accepted as an entrant for the 60th Anniversary of the 2022 Koestler Arts Exhibition within three categories including 'Fine Art'. My beloved birth son James is now over 21 and is 100% independent of my formal guardian responsibility role. My half acre in Jamaica was for a time categorised as a Religious Society of Friends 'Quaker Space' where it was also permitted to fly drones and use robotics via Bluetooth. I remain a unapologetic Apple addict and became formally commercially trained as a Drone Pilot and owner of mainly DJI Drones inclusive of the spark, phantom pro and Mavic Pro, added to my fleet is a GoPro Karma Drone and tiny Holy Stone drone. I was trained by the CAA civil aviation authorities approved 'Uplift Drones' registered company and Before I retired from Thames Reach homelessness Charity I wrote and published the Apple book 'My Granny is a drone pilot'. It is a short Childrens book which adults can read which I have dedicated to my grandchildren. I have one grandchild. A granddaughter. She is the bloodline birth granddaughter of my much loved black Jamaican woman Jamaica constabulary Force Police Officer and there is NO woman alive I love more than her. I am a stocks and shares holder and own a few shares in Apple, BP and Marks and Spencer's… to name a few. I was a named director of a few Companies House limited businesses and once held a formal mortgage for a three bedroom London house at 95 Highclere Street, Sydenham.

I remain a London born Londoner and usually resident in a housing cooperative rented maisonette in Brixton, Windrush Ward Lambeth; where I resided whilst conducting my lived experience Rethink Mental Illness 'Schizophrenia Commission' commissioner role and Stonewall UK 'Schools Role model' voluntary work. It has also been the address on the ballot paper for all of the elections I stood for within the 'Coldharbour Ward' including my last 2018 By Election. All for The Tory Conservatives.

Photographs from the start

1. Me & my son James

2. Paul Burstow MP &me

3. My son James, me & my same sex partner Julian
4. Prime minister David Cameron & me

5. Me & Rufus May

6. Me & Jonny Benjamin MBE

7. Nornan Lamb MP, me & Deputy Prime minister Nick Clegg

8. Diane Abbott MP & me

9. Me & Justine Greening MP

10. Me & Sir Ian McKellen 11. Me
12. Me & Alan Broomhead Chairman of DWNCA -Dulwich & West Norwood Conservatives Association
13. Two Stonewall employees & me

14. Ken Olisa, Thames Reach Chairman, me & Jeremy Swain, Thames Reach CEO/Chief Executive
15. Me & Chair of DWNCA WAGs -Women's Action Group

16.   Me at my full time paid Waterloo Project, Thames Reach employment

17.   Me, my same sex partner Julian & my son James at the Sugar Bay Resort in Barbados
18.   Rev'd Sharon Ferguson & me

19.   My same sex partner Julian, me & my son James on holiday in Barbados
20.   Me & one of my former Mental Health Care Coordinators
21.   Me & Matthew Patrick CEO/Chief Executive of SLAM - South London & Maudsley Psychiatric Hospital NHS - National Health Service Trust
22.   Me & Unknown Person

23.   Laura Sandy MP & me

24.   My son James & me

25.   Donotus & me

26.   Me & Time to Change activists

27.   Guillaine & Me

28.   Councillor Jacqui Dyer MBE & me

29.   My same sex partner Julian & me

30.   My son James & my Jehovah's Witness mother; Sister Lilian Brown in Luton, Bedfordshire

31. My same sex partner Julian & my son James
32. My son James & me

33. Me

34. Me

35. Me & the first openly Gay Mayor of Liverpool
36. Me

37. Sue Baker OBE & me

38. Alistair Campbell, me & Time to Change Activist
39. Me & Syed Kamall MEP

40. Me

41. Me at my DWNCA Executive Members Meeting [Photograph taken by me]
42. Me & my Brompton Bicycle

43. Birgit Rapp - my best female friend.

www.ingramcontent.com/pod-product-compliance
Lightning Source LLC
Chambersburg PA
CBHW050847240426
43667CB00022B/2952